FAIRFIELD PUBLIC LIBRARY
261 HOLLYWOOD AVENUE
FAIRFIELD, NEW JERSEY 07004
973-227-3575

A VISIT TO
FRANCE

Story by Kirsten Hall
Illustrated by Benrei Huang

A GOLDEN BOOK • NEW YORK
Western Publishing Company, Inc. Racine, Wisconsin 53404

© 1991 Nancy Hall, Inc. Illustrations © 1991 Benrei Huang. All rights reserved. Printed in the U.S.A. No part of this book may be reproduced or copied in any form without written permission from the publisher. All trademarks are the property of Western Publishing Company, Inc. Developed by Nancy Hall, Inc. Library of Congress Catalog Card Number: 90-85683 ISBN: 0-307-12630-7/ ISBN: 0-307-62630-X (lib. bdg.) A MCMXCI

Lucas and Raphael Duval are brothers who live in Paris, France. Lucas is seven, and Raphael is twelve years old. They live with their mother in an apartment on the Right Bank of the Seine River.

Tomorrow is Mama's birthday. "What should we get for her?" asked Lucas as the boys were getting ready for bed.
"I've been thinking about that all week," replied Raphael, "but I can't think of anything that's really special."

The next morning the boys woke up to a beautiful summer day. The sun was shining brightly, and the streets were full of Saturday morning merchants.

But today the boys had only one thing on their minds. They knew that their mother would be very busy at her studio all day preparing for an important art exhibition.

"We have a lot to do today, Luc," said Raphael. "While Mama is at work, we must find the perfect present."

While they were getting dressed, Mama called them for breakfast.

Their mother had put out a traditional French breakfast—bread, *croissants*, and jam. Hot chocolate was warming on the stove.

"Happy birthday, Mama!" they shouted as they ran to give her a big hug.

"Thank you, boys," said Mama happily, pouring hot chocolate into their cups.

They finished their breakfast quickly and Lucas grabbed a *croissant* to take along.

"Good-bye!" they called as they prepared to leave.

"Wait!" their mother called back. "Meet me at the *Tuileries* garden at five o'clock. And don't be late for lunch at Uncle Pierre's."

The boys kissed their mother good-bye and hurried down the stairs.

As they ran down the street they passed their favorite *crêperie,* where they often stopped after school. The owner was turning over chairs in preparation for his morning customers. He waved to Raphael and Lucas.

"Good morning, boys! Can you spare a few moments to help?" he asked.

"We are looking for a present for Mother's birthday," Raphael answered, "but I suppose we could help you first."

"If you do," the owner added, "I'll give you some freshly baked *baguettes* for your trouble."

When they had finished, as promised, the owner thanked them and handed them three little loaves of French bread.

The boys continued on their way. They stopped at several shops in the neighborhood. But nothing seemed special enough to buy.

They passed many beautiful buildings, including the *Arc de Triomphe,* a large monument built by Napoleon to symbolize France's military victories. It stands at the top of the *Avenue des Champs Elysées,* and the *Louvre,* one of the most famous museums in the world, is at the far end.

"We should be able to find something here," said Lucas as they headed down the long avenue crowded with shops and restaurants. They peeked in window after window. But everything they liked was too expensive. When they reached the *Louvre,* they still had no present for their mother. "We'd better head over to Uncle Pierre's for lunch," said Raphael.

A few blocks down the street they saw their uncle's *épicerie,* a small grocery store. As they got closer they noticed Robert, one of the clerks, struggling to bring in some large cartons that had just been delivered. Raphael and Lucas offered to help.

"Why, thank you, boys!" Robert replied. When the work was finished, he rewarded them with a bag full of fresh fruit and several kinds of cheese.

The boys walked through the *épicerie* to the little apartment in the back. Uncle Pierre, Aunt Marie, and their cousin Michel, who was sixteen, were waiting for them. Hungry from all the walking they had done, they were delighted to smell *ratatouille* cooking on the stove. As they ate the delicious casserole of eggplant, tomatoes, peppers, onions, and zucchini, Lucas complained about how discouraged he was.

"Everything we saw cost too much," explained Raphael.

"Well," said Michel, "your mama loves paintings. I could take you to *Montmartre* and see if we can find something. A lot of artists show their work there."

"Great!" they agreed, thanking Michel for his offer.

Michel took Raphael and Lucas on the *Metro*, the Paris subway. They got off when they reached the stop for *Montmartre*.

Weaving in and out of the narrow streets, they stopped to look at sidewalk artists and visited galleries full of beautiful things. There was only one problem—again, everything they liked cost too much.

"We should have started saving our money sooner," said Raphael. "Then we might have had enough to get Mama something beautiful!"

"I like Mama's paintings better than these, anyway," said Lucas, who was trying to cheer up his brother.

Tired from all of their walking, and not sure what to do next, the boys sat down to rest in front of a *charcuterie*, a delicatessen that specializes in fine meats. Raphael looked inside at the case full of sausages and sliced hams. Then he looked at their bags filled with *baguettes* and fruit and cheese.

"I have an idea!" he said happily. He rushed to the counter and carefully chose an assortment of delicious meats.

"What are you doing?" asked Lucas.

"You'll see," said Raphael with a smile as he led Lucas and Michel out of the store. Then he went next door to the *pâtisserie,* where he bought eclairs and tarts and other sweets.

"But now we have only a few *francs* left!" complained Lucas.

"And no present," added Michel.

"Wrong," said Raphael. "Let's find a *supermarché*. We have just enough money to get the one thing we still need."

Raphael explained his plan, and the three set out to find the final touch.

At five o'clock, Michel dropped the boys off at the front of the *Tuileries*. Their mother was waiting at the entrance to the gardens.

"My, my! What have we here?" she asked. The boys' faces peeked out from behind their packages.

"Lots of treats for you, Mama!" cried Lucas happily. "We even got a special tablecloth—the final touch!"

Lucas helped Raphael with the tablecloth.

"A picnic in the garden!" said their mother. "What a wonderful idea! You must have been working on this all day!" Then together they shared the bread, fruit, cheese, sausage, ham, and pastries. The boys smiled happily. They both agreed this was the best birthday surprise ever.

Facts About France

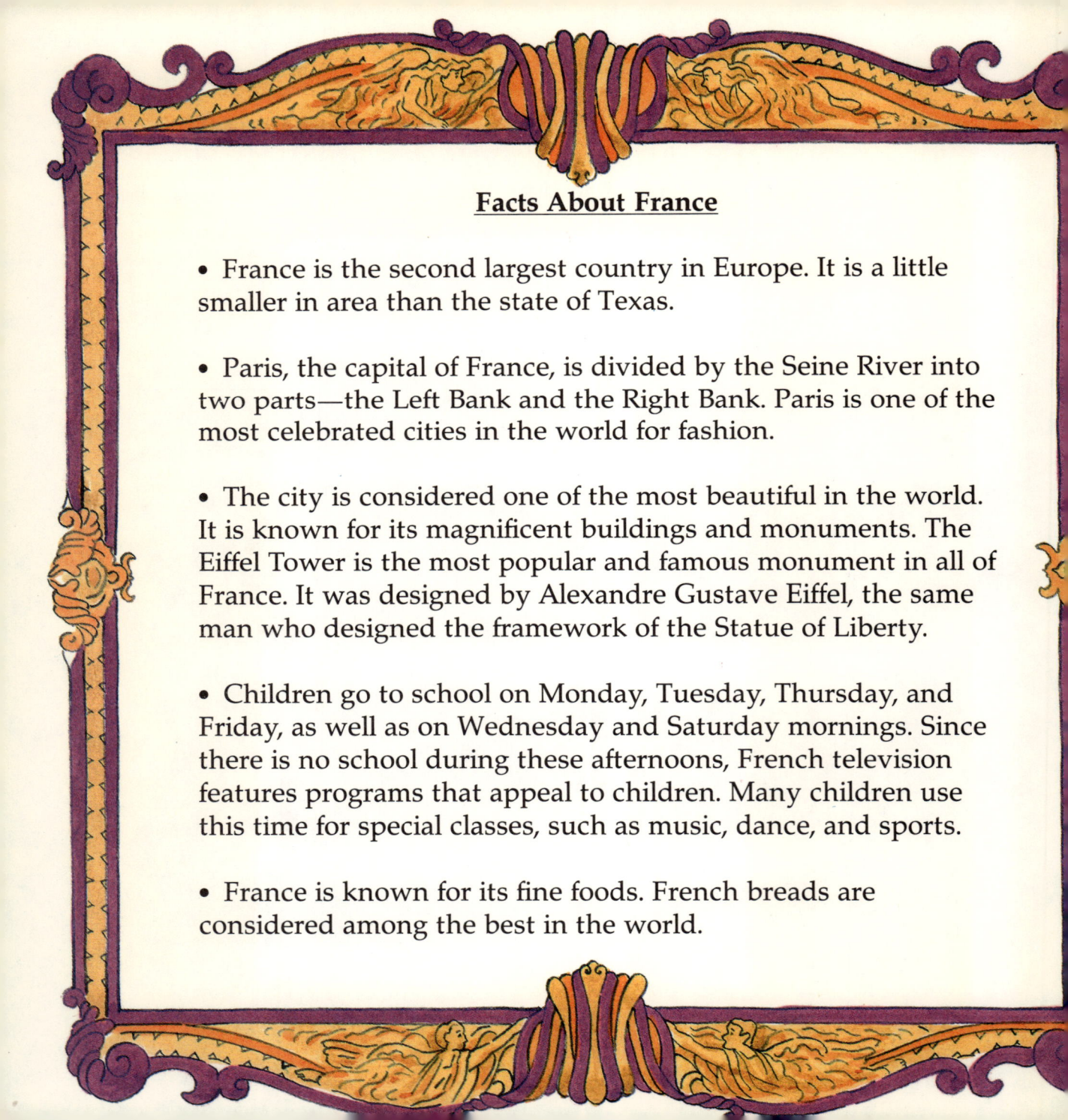

- France is the second largest country in Europe. It is a little smaller in area than the state of Texas.

- Paris, the capital of France, is divided by the Seine River into two parts—the Left Bank and the Right Bank. Paris is one of the most celebrated cities in the world for fashion.

- The city is considered one of the most beautiful in the world. It is known for its magnificent buildings and monuments. The Eiffel Tower is the most popular and famous monument in all of France. It was designed by Alexandre Gustave Eiffel, the same man who designed the framework of the Statue of Liberty.

- Children go to school on Monday, Tuesday, Thursday, and Friday, as well as on Wednesday and Saturday mornings. Since there is no school during these afternoons, French television features programs that appeal to children. Many children use this time for special classes, such as music, dance, and sports.

- France is known for its fine foods. French breads are considered among the best in the world.

920647

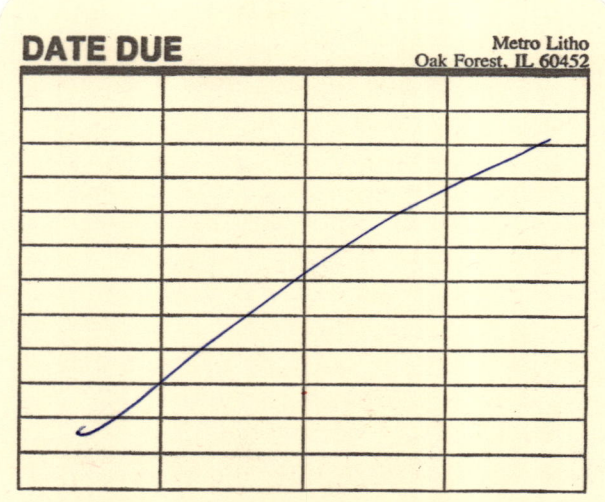

E   Hall, Kirsten
HA   A visit to France

FAIRFIELD PUBLIC LIBRARY
261 HOLLYWOOD AVENUE
FAIRFIELD, NEW JERSEY 07004
973-227-3575